WHAT

HAVE

I

TO

SAY

TO

YOU

WHAT HAVE I TO SAY TO YOU

Megan Levad

TAVERN BOOKS

PORTLAND

Copyright © 2017 Megan Levad.
All rights reserved.
Printed in the United States of America.

Tavern Books receives support from the Oregon Arts Commission, a state agency funded by the State of Oregon.

The author wishes to thank: the editors of *Poetry Northwest* ("Reader, I have of late come into a dictatorship" and "The agricultural industrial complex turns to me at karaoke") and *Sierra Nevada Review* ("My love is a fungus," "You think it's over," and "Your mother turns to me at the seafood restaurant"); composer Dominick DiOrio; several kind readers of the manuscript at various stages, including Julie Babcock, Paul Beisner, Jennifer Metsker, Jorge Sánchez, Stephanie Soileau, Kerri Webster, and Jacqueline Williams; and The Rice Place and the MacDowell Colony, for their generous residencies.

Cover art: Natasha Molotkova, *Dodo*, 2015. Quilled currency.
Copyright © Natasha Molotkova. Courtesy of the artist.

Levad, Megan, 1978 -

ISBN-13: 978-1-935635-76-5 (paperback)
ISBN-13: 978-1-935635-77-2 (hardcover)

LCCN: 2017942206

FIRST EDITION

98765432 First Printing

TAVERN BOOKS
Union Station
800 NW 6th Avenue #255
Portland, Oregon 97209
www.tavernbooks.org

The stain of love

is upon the world.

>—William Carlos Williams
>from "A Love Song"

I LIE HERE THINKING OF YOU

Thinking of you is dreaming

I lie here dreaming

I HAVE TAKEN A VOW

not to use a simile
or metaphor

when I speak of our love

I want it to be itself
and nothing else

So Lover
Reader

you will have to get used to
my close, brothy stink
and the chill of the examination table

YOUR MOTHER TURNS TO ME
in your childhood bedroom, says

It's going to be
62 degrees on Saturday

She puts away your shirts
She checks your drawers

for chewing gum

What did we do to deserve that?

She leaves
your pebbles, feather, rubber band

a letter to your older self
on the nightstand

We're gonna pay for it later

READER,

When you read these words
your brain makes

the same grooves
mine did
when I wrote them

So when I say

I am inside you
I am part of your chimeric body

if body is what
we call the whole
collection

I mean, I'm not not

The heat I feel I feel
all the way

over there in my body

I watch while
eighteen hundred parents

stand for the Hallelujah
chorus in a college gymnasium

From here I see it
my body

waving to you
like wheat in the wind

coarse, plain, alive

under the sun
like everything

WE DON'T SAY THINGS LIKE
I will find you

You can go to any snug corner
of the globe

and I will find you

I have trained
a mute of hounds to bay

when they find you

I have taught my falcons to carry
a drop of your blood

I will find you, my darling

My horses travel
for days without flagging

I am crafty
and relentless as a Hun

The wolves, whales, tall ships
bear traps

and moonlight
are all on our side, dear

I will find you

No, we don't say things like that
anymore

Reader,

I have a bad feeling
about all this

YOUR DENTIST TURNS TO ME
in the county courthouse, says

*Happy family or unhappy
what difference does it make?*

Outside, an elderly
woman fed the pigeons
day-old rolls

until a policeman
strode up

threatened to ticket

In the time it takes
to remember

what sort of hat was fashionable
in the 1940s

the clerk changes
my name to yours

Some leaves taste like tea

Large and docile

animals can be
yoked, milked

Other presences
invisible filaments

web through our best bread

Knowing this
I want to stammer for you

some lines about electricity

but all that comes is
love's the burning boy

I SEE YOU
without clothes

for me

your long weekend
body, my dangerous smell

our nipples like your mother's

Don't worry, God can't hear us

READER,

It feels good
to promise you things

Your county sheriff turns to me
at the seafood restaurant, says

After I met him
but before he was

my husband, my husband
didn't call for three weeks

I sort of forgot about him

I ask if by then
they had already

married and divorced
in her mind

but she doesn't hear

She's replaced her old face
with a new one

Your gender studies professor turns to me
in the elevator to the 42nd floor, says

Tight in the butt and not see-through

We've been talking
about loungewear

yogapants
the loss of longjohns

She's explaining
the appeal of a woman

in a rough morning braid
and a union suit

while I click through my to-dos
shopping lists

my shame a constant hum

Somehow the human race
has managed despite

*the only very recent
invention of the bikini wax*

And somehow we think
oral sex was a 20th-century idea

*But people are people and people
want what people want*

Ding

We step into the penthouse
still
in our same bodies

HIGH SCHOOL FOOTBALL TURNS TO ME
in the Dairy Queen parking lot, says

But what about Wagner?

We are eating
vanilla soft-serve

I usually order cherry dip

but since he treated
I got what he was having

His mouth is ringed white

It smells like the inside
of a new refrigerator

I think he's ready to attack

READER,

I will be up front with you

My wife is away
next weekend

and I'm looking
for something to do

Not sexual
it's just been so long

since I told my old stories
to someone new

Sometimes when we're together
I can't tell

if I'm more like a robot
or an animal

When I try to describe it
to a friend

I say there's no time
I say I am outside

the comfort of
a future

I say there never was
a future

Count with me

sidewalks, raincoats, podcasts, salads
the hours and hours alone

When I try to describe it
to a friend

I say there's
no ground under me

I say
I am outside the order

I say
there never was an order

What I mean is
the laws of physics

are a story, too

as much as mine
with you

I'm saying
gravity only works

by agreement, suspension
of disbelief

You can tell me
anything you like

when I finally
let go

Today I read about ducks
how much ducks love rape

then spent an hour
in an online search for

an unlined bra

I want my nipples
to show

I want to feel
the chalky friction

of two layers
softcup, blouse

against my breasts

I think about it
while I get dressed

ducks, bras

and the woman

in the stairwell

who thought she'd just had
one of those rare

erotic encounters
with a stranger

fast, unpleasant, adult

and about the man
in the stairwell

who went away thinking
he'd raped her

I think about her
dressing that morning

and desire, I think
about desire

Reader,

If you feed me
I'll forget how to feed myself

I have no one to talk to
I am my own Texas

I am a stadium
filled with screaming fans

I have no one to talk to

I am Amelia Earhart
piloting the Kittyhawk

with the Lindbergh baby
strapped to my chest

I am first in everything

I am a career violinist

The bruise on my neck
I did it to myself

Reader,

The news from this country

weather, stock prices

closely follows
that of your own

Every front and surge
is a message

Hollywood turns to me
in the grocery line, says

She could hold two lies
in her mouth at once

before the crown of her head
unfolds like a mourning

dove and flies away

I like to wear your clothes

and not just because
I like that mask

I want to ask
how you feel
with me

in your closet
your bathtub

your love
your country

your treehouse
your trunk

No. I want
you
to ask
me

Online dating turns to me
from the climbing wall, says

*I'm all laid back
like a hippie on a yoga mat*

She's up there pretty high

The footholds

pumpkin, hambone, black walnut
sequins
even close up

are motes
from down here

and I am the someone, somewhere
holding the rope

VEGANISM TURNS TO ME
at the cafe, says

*This green tea latte
tastes like truth!*

But I am caught up
in a scheme

and nothing has tasted
like truth

since the last time
I shot clays with you

Reader,

I'm sorry I can't be
more helpful

I'm only
an assistant

My love is
a Christmas tree farm

set aflame
by two kids with wild minds

and my love is
the flask of bourbon

the apple
and the matchbook

and my love is
the wet spot

on the scarf
where breath melts

MY LOVE IS
a fungus

hidden a few inches underground
or in the air's plain sight

only fruiting for a few hours

after a rain

Given a whole day
to meditate

on your beauty

I come up with
a tacky fishing lure

of bobs and dangles

cherry pie
beaver skin
the smell of cold wool
some foxing

held together
on a bright blond line

Your line was always

That's right

since I gave it to you
the right, that is

to tell me
what is

The Beauty of Your Beauty

is that I don't see it
your beauty

The tight flesh
that naps your nose

the color
of blood

that shies out
from under your cheeks

the ends of your
fingers whorled

Okay. I'm beginning
to agree with them

your face
fits your face

and it fits
your open palms

Your face fits
my open palms, too

Prosperity Christianity turns to me
at the veterinarian's office, says

She got together with
her high-school boyfriend

The cat spits pink medicine
all over the vet's assistant

Her kids are having a real
hard time with it

I STILL LOVE YOU
so much

if I met you again
I'd have to kill you

for your pelt

The psychos
aren't wrong

They can't help it
They're appendices

tailbones, vestigial
parts of a much longer history

a history
as long as ours

My innocence
is sinister

It sees
the evil

that isn't there

Reader,

My heart is broken

which means
it doesn't work anymore

even if it's wound
every night

The Rust Belt turns to me
at the strip mall sports bar, says

Am I going to die?

I tell him to finish
his turkey burger

and motion to
the waitress

young and lovely
tits on a stick

for the check

*If I manage my affairs correctly
it will be like I was never here*

Reader,

I have of late
come into a dictatorship

The country is perhaps
only eight by ten

but rich with building materials
strange birds

and ornamental grasses

I have found myself
to possess a natural talent

for the work

IN THAT SCENARIO
I think I would

save your mother

you would get
the fifty-fifty

I would drown

the most romantic
way to go

But I might be wrong

gun to my head
I tend to mess up

orphan or widow

I waver, my limbs taffy
my mouth starts

to digest
my teeth

THE AGRICULTURAL INDUSTRIAL COMPLEX TURNS TO ME
at the karaoke bar, says

The man loved making commitments

I picture a heart
overflowing

with tight scrolls
appointments scribbled

on each one

Goddammit
Somebody already did "Jolene"

light pencil, fine hand

Reader,

This year's spiders
have more horrible faces

and day jobs

I can only afford to keep them
down here

for an hour a night

Please think of that hour
as a signifier for the whole night

Reader,

My nation is
an autonomy

But I promise
there's room

enough for two

just do as I say
and do as you say too

Reader,

Sometimes I wish
you had killed

yourself, instead

It would be easier
to believe that
when you said

it's not my fault

you meant it

I LOVE YOU MORE
than God loves you

and like God
I love myself still more

all existence

contingent upon
my existence

I AM PREPARED

high-quality inflatable mattress
peppermint castile soap

hand-crank flashlight-slash-radio
gallons and gallons of water

I have filled the first aid kit
with bandages and salves

Come, radiant bridegroom
all is ready

I don't care
if we have to go back

so far that our skulls thicken
grow slope-browed and narrow

heavy

I want to get to
the bottom of it

Reader,

When this is all over
I think we should go

have our hymens
surgically reconstructed

Or we could get
Coney dogs

I just want to spend
the day with you

I NEVER LIED

any expectations
are your own responsibility

but I am a generous boss

so whatever you mistook
may be returned

to the locker
under the stairs

I wrote the combination
on the waterline

of your left eyelid
as you slept

You know, we're friends now
so we should split the check

Reader,

Only when free
from projections

can we be aware
of reality

You are sensitive
sympathetic and considerate

You have a strong desire
for home and family

Your next interview
will result in a job

AFTER THE LAST SKEIN OF GEESE
bossed through overhead

I went inside

Now the circle
we've drawn

around us
sounds like

space

which is to say the polite
clink of blood cells

queueing in quiet chains

MARKETABLE NOSTALGIA TURNS TO ME
in the private library, says

Suicides never consider
Who am I doing this to?

My first thought is
To whom am I doing this

and then I realize
my reconstruction

makes the suicide
an actor, self-murderer

He touches a hard gilt
spine with one finger

My sorrow is chthonic
a choir of lowing whales

could not move the stone
I've set upon it

When a compass
is broken

it can be replaced

needle, cork, shallow dish
is all it takes

More difficult
is learning

the compass is broken

That part takes decades
of wandering in the desert

Reader,

Remember
all of this

takes place in bed

BECAUSE YOU WORK SO HARD
I punish myself

make the day
a tight plait

garden, market, stiff rows
of clean dishes

office, jogging
inbox zero

I tick off the seconds
under my breath

wait for you
to find me worthy

complete, incorruptible
sound throughout

Neoliberalism turns to me
at the apothecary, says

He was my Starbuck

She is color-matched
to Radiant

while I dimple the rubber
dropper tops

with my forefinger

If we could stay
I would time them

see which ones pop first

but I still wouldn't
know why

He could comply
but he could never agree

There's no other way
to explain it

What grown-ass man
dresses up in a costume

or types love letters
in all caps?

Only someone
unforgivable

in his excitement

Reader,

When I bite
it's true

I want to
hurt you

I am
like the tiger

who murders
her trainer

unable to understand
cause and effect

or permanence

HUMANITIES EDUCATION TURNS TO ME
at the auto shop, says

*My sadness bears
no relation to sadness*

I am about to correct her, say
it's happiness

she means, but we are not
reciting poems

We're talking about
satisfaction and her losses

the son, the house
the best linen dress

I am about to correct her, say
something

ephemeral about the ephemeral

when the mechanic
gives his diagnosis

I'll run it into the ground

THE GREATEST GENERATION TURNS TO ME
in a parked car, says

*Do you think that's why
the hippies beat up soldiers*

*even drafted guys?
Because they lost the war?*

I look through binoculars
and try to find the nest

Peregrine falcons
eyasses

I'm supposed to watch them
feed on pigeons

She points, I look
to her hand

and lose the tree
once more

WHEN YOU DIE
I can fall

in love
all over again

I'll see you everywhere

like when we first met

I miss that time
It was dismissed

as sexual obsession
but now we know it for

the mourning practice
it was

THE SUSPENSION OF HABEAS CORPUS TURNS TO ME
at the racetrack, says

*I'm going to wear cutoffs to work
every day until I get my raise*

Before I can suggest
a more efficient strategy

she's got her hat
in the air

*You know all the jockeys are
Mexicans now*

You should see her
when she's all riled up

Is my tan rubbing off?

If she's ever been
more beautiful

prove it

Reader,

when we're watching sports

and there's little sports
inside the big sports

I like it when you're
the big sports

Systemic racism turns to me
in the elementary school hallway, says

Even her smileyfaces were wrong

I am distracted
by convention

Who uses an equal sign for the eyes?

and grammar

glamor's clever
little sister

Say these words
in this order

*It's narcissistic, being
that out of step*

It's a spell

He won't know
what hit him

I miss you so much
that I miss you right now

As you wade
down the creek

in those cheap peachskin pants
beautiful, exactly

the heart's spine curls

I want to talk to you
when I'm talking to you

WE MET IN A PAST LIFE
I think

shared a taxi
You: maybe

British, vaguely authoritative
Me: me

We were chambermaids maybe
people who knew

What I like about you is—

doesn't matter

It's not like
I worried about being born

before I was born

Reader,

I admit
I am overdue

for a bang trim

I know I know
my hair is in your eyes

THE GLOBAL ECONOMY TURNS TO ME
at barre class, says

*Can you explain dialectical materialism
in two to three sentences?*

I know that
I know a joke about this

too much coal, not enough coal

but I have to concentrate
so hard on my ass muscles

in order to get through this set
I don't say anything

I shake my head
Appropriate and expected

stars of sweat
shine on her brow

Come on, you can do it

AMERICA TURNS TO ME
at the oyster bar, says

*I've always been vain
about my low affect*

She's painted her lips
Freshly Fucked Pink

and now she's parting
her eyelashes

with a straight pin

*If you want to be friends with him
be friends with him*

I start again
with my explanation

but she's impassive
about to suck down another

I WANT THINGS
to be different

I want to be
that fugitive

I mean, that future self
again

I didn't get to see
what would happen

The experiment has ended

There will be no results

Abstract Expressionism turns to me
at the dog park, says

I told him if you have bed memories
move the bed

His gaze is gentle
on a sticky-looking boy

wilted mohawk, iced mocha
notebook

Take that kid for example

Near the chainlink
a woman in big shorts
ties herself to a pit bull

Write everything down
and of course you'll remember
things you wish you didn't

EVOLUTIONARY PSYCHOLOGY TURNS TO ME
at the reading of *Antigone*, says

That Kreon turns me on

I think she means
authority, its unabashed security

opens imaginative possibilities
by which she means her legs

not that she admires
this actor

wonders at him
the magic

of middle-aged salt-and-pepper
with a Magnum 'stache

and a paper crown

Military hegemony turns to me
at the municipal pool, says

This is like a mini-vacation, isn't it?

While the veiled women lower
their soft pantlegs into the water

her swim-blue suit
slips from her shoulder

she fixes her nipple

Isn't it? Like a mini-vacation?

AND SO I BEGAN A ROMANCE
with myself

In this way
I am protected

scrimmed off
in my brittle white robe

magnificent with loneliness

a prairie fire
seen underwater

from space

in a mirror

Reader,

Now turn around

I want us
to do this

with your ass
in my face

Monogamy turns to me
in the treehouse, says

*She smelled like peaches
and old books*

A football toss
between a young woman

in crushed velvet pajamas
and a man

in aviator sunglasses
swings below us

No one is watching the baby

Moldy, wholesome

YOU THINK IT'S OVER

but now we have all these
radioactive sites

to protect
forever or until

some other apocalypse

THE COLLECTIVE UNCONSCIOUS TURNS TO ME
at the cineplex, says

Junior Mints or Swedish Fish?

His eyes glitter
with the melancholy

of a three-day hangover

He wanted to see
the new Batman

who looks like
the old Batman to me

The satisfaction of rejection
is more perfect

than any fantasy
of complete union

Speak of the devil

my old self
would have chosen
Junior Mints

If you never read this
I will have to

point to the shape of you
in the pressèd grass

And even if now, somewhere
you are happy

even if you still
watch your coffee drip

and think
of me

I don't know
that to be certain

so it's as good
as false

I might as well sing
my songs into the shower hose

Loss turns to me
at the ballet recital, says

*He was always the tallest
kid in his class*

We are watching six-year-olds
in neon green capri pants

dance individual tangoes
to "Love Me or Leave Me"

She is watching through her camera
I through my eyes

Young Nina Simone
breaks into blossom

and the teacher does the dance
small in the wing

*So now he looks
a little unfinished*

When I said I wanted
to be buried with your people

I meant with you

I don't want to be left alone
with them

for eternity

We would have
grown bored

This no-man's land
for two

the every, every
day of it

Eventually we would have
had to

release our balloons
a prayer

that somebody else
is out there

Wait, listen—

Reader,

When I wake
from all this

in the cave
of your curved body

my wristwatch on the nightstand
please know

I meant everything I said

I stomped your name
into the dirt

letters taller
than wooden gods
and visible from Mars

You're never getting
out of here

Love turns to me
at the oxygen bar, says

I'm going to miss my flight

Our toxins
are being replaced

with lavender
and chamomile

*I hope he parks
not circles*

Either way
I'm traveling alone

About the Author

Megan Levad is the author of *Why We Live in the Dark Ages,* the first selection in Tavern Books' Wrolstad Contemporary Poetry Series. A recent MacDowell fellow, her poems have appeared in *Tin House, Granta Online, Fence,* and the Everyman's Library anthology *Killer Verse,* among other publications. She also writes lyrics and libretti; her first opera, *Kept,* with composer Kristin Kuster, premiered in May 2017.

Tavern Books

Tavern Books is a not-for-profit poetry publisher that exists to print, promote, and preserve works of literary vision, to foster a climate of cultural preservation, and to disseminate books in a way that benefits the reading public.

We publish books in translation from the world's finest poets, champion new works by innovative writers, and revive out-of-print classics. We keep our titles in print, honoring the cultural contract between publisher and author, as well as between publisher and public. Our catalog, known as The Living Library, sustains the visions of our authors, ensuring their voices remain alive in the social and artistic discourse of our modern era.

Subscriptions

Become a subscriber and receive the next six Tavern Books titles at a substantial discount, delivered to your door. Paperback and hardcover subscriptions available.

For details visit www.tavernbooks.org/subscriptions or write to us at:

Tavern Books
at Union Station
800 NW 6th Avenue #255
Portland, Oregon 97209

The Living Library

Killing Floor by Ai

Arthur's Talk with the Eagle by Anonymous,
translated from the Welsh by Gwyneth Lewis

Ashulia by Zubair Ahmed

Breckinridge County Suite by Joe Bolton

My People & Other Poems by Wojciech Bonowicz,
translated from the Polish by Piotr Florczyk

Who Lives by Elisabeth Borchers,
translated from the German by Caroline Wilcox Reul

Buson: Haiku by Yosa Buson,
translated from the Japanese by Franz Wright

Poems 1904 by C.P. Cavafy,
translated from the Greek by Paul Merchant

Evidence of What Is Said by Ann Charters and Charles Olson

Who Whispered Near Me by Killarney Clary

The End of Space by Albert Goldbarth

Six-Minute Poems: The Last Poems
by George Hitchcock

The Wounded Alphabet: Collected Poems
by George Hitchcock

Hitchcock on Trial
by George Hitchcock

At the Devil's Banquets by Anise Koltz,
translated from the French by John F. Deane

My Blue Piano by Else Lasker-Schüler,
translated from the German by Eavan Boland

What Have I to Say to You by Megan Levad

Why We Live in the Dark Ages by Megan Levad

Archeology by Adrian C. Louis

Fire Water World & Among the Dog Eaters
by Adrian C. Louis

Emergency Brake by Ruth Madievsky

Under an Arkansas Sky by Jo McDougall

The Undiscovered Room by Jo McDougall

Ocean by Joseph Millar

Petra by Amjad Nasser,
translated from the Arabic by Fady Joudah

The Fire's Journey: Part I by Eunice Odio,
translated from the Spanish by Keith Ekiss
with Sonia P. Ticas and Mauricio Espinoza

The Fire's Journey: Part II by Eunice Odio,
translated from the Spanish by Keith Ekiss
with Sonia P. Ticas and Mauricio Espinoza

**The Fire's Journey: Part III* by Eunice Odio,
translated from the Spanish by Keith Ekiss
with Sonia P. Ticas and Mauricio Espinoza

The Fire's Journey: Part IV by Eunice Odio,
translated from the Spanish by Keith Ekiss
with Sonia P. Ticas and Mauricio Espinoza

Full Body Pleasure Suit by Elsbeth Pancrazi

Duino Elegies by Rainer Maria Rilke,
translated from the German by Gary Miranda

Twelve Poems About Cavafy by Yannis Ritsos,
translated from the Greek by Paul Merchant

Monochords by Yannis Ritsos,
translated from the Greek by Paul Merchant

Glowing Enigmas by Nelly Sachs,
translated from the German by Michael Hamburger

Prodigy by Charles Simic,
drawings by Charles Seluzicki

Night of Shooting Stars by Leonardo Sinisgalli,
translated from the Italian by W. S. Di Piero

Skin by Tone Škrjanec,
translated from the Slovene by Matthew Rohrer and Ana Pepelnik

We Women by Edith Södergran,
translated from the Swedish by Samuel Charters

Winterward by William Stafford

Building the Barricade by Anna Świrszczyńska,
translated from the Polish by Piotr Florczyk

Baltics by Tomas Tranströmer,
with photographs by Ann Charters,
translated from the Swedish by Samuel Charters

For the Living and the Dead by Tomas Tranströmer,
translated from the Swedish by John F. Deane

Prison: Nine Haiku from Hällby Youth Prison by Tomas Tranströmer,
translated from the Swedish by Malena Mörling

Tomas Tranströmer's First Poems & Notes from the Land of Lap Fever
by Tomas Tranströmer and Jonas Ellerström,
translated from the Swedish by Malena Mörling

Collected Translations by David Wevill

Casual Ties by David Wevill

Where the Arrow Falls by David Wevill

A Christ of the Ice-Floes by David Wevill

Night Is Simply a Shadow by Greta Wrolstad

Notes on Sea & Shore by Greta Wrolstad

The Countries We Live In by Natan Zach,
translated from the Hebrew by Peter Everwine

*forthcoming

Tavern Books is funded, in part, by the generosity of philanthropic organizations, public and private institutions, and individual donors. By supporting Tavern Books and its mission, you enable us to publish the most exciting poets from around the world. To learn more about underwriting Tavern Books titles, please contact us by e-mail: info@tavernbooks.org.

MAJOR FUNDING HAS BEEN PROVIDED BY

OREGON ARTS COMMISSION

Lannan

THE LIBRA FOUNDATION

THE PUBLICATION OF THIS BOOK IS MADE POSSIBLE, IN PART, BY THE SUPPORT OF THE FOLLOWING INDIVIDUALS

Sophie Cabot Black
Joe Bratcher
Dean & Karen Garyet
Daniel Handler
Kate Harbour
Jennifer Jones & Mark Swartz
Leah Middlebrook
Joseph Millar & Dorianne Laux
Jay Ponteri

Mary Ann Ryan
Donna Swartz
Mary Szybist & Jerry Harp
Bill & Leah Stenson
Jonathan Wells
Dan Wieden
Wendy Willis & David Biespiel
Vince & Patty Wixon
Ron & Kathy Wrolstad

Colophon

This book was designed and typeset by Eldon Potter at Bryan Potter Design, Portland, Oregon. Text is set in Garamond, an old-style serif typeface named for the punch-cutter Claude Garamond (c. 1480-1561). *What Have I to Say to You* appears in both paperback and cloth-covered editions. Printed on archival-quality paper by McNaughton & Gunn, Inc.